# The Pillars for Global Catharsis

Dr. Edward Schellhammer

**The Pillars For Global Catharsis.**
**1st Edition, 2017.**
© **Copyright. Dr. Edward Schellhammer.**

**ISBN-13: 978-1975857431**
**ISBN-10: 1975857437**

**www.EdwardSchellhammer.com**
**www.SchellhammerBusinessSchool.com**
**www.SchellhammerInstitute.com**
**www.SchellhammerRetreat.com**

# TABLE OF CONTENTS

# 1. EARLY POSITIVE MIND SHAPING

Meditative regressions unveiled:

- A fetus has a soul; the soul (an energetic body) has a natural (also energetic) ability to perceive external realities.

- A fetus recognizes the truth even though the state of brain development does not yet fully understand such perceptions.

- The soul of a fetus also has a general scale for what is good and bad (evil) as an instinctive part of self-preservation.

*A fetus has a natural basic conscience (disposition/need), to be obviously developed through the manifold mental functions (mind).*

All humans therefore already have immense mental

potential to be developed during prenatal time and especially during the first 5 years of their life. Fact is however that a huge majority of parents do not care for the development of their children's potentials. This is also proof that they do not care for the future of their children, which means in the end that they do not love their children. They do not know how to care because they have experienced the same resulting in the vicious downward spiral of degenerative evolution.

Early good experiences:

Peace, happiness, love and all positive experiences (e.g. music, wellbeing, learning stimulations and talking to the fetus/infant) stimulate the brain and mind development during both prenatal and postnatal time. Supportive factors are:

☺   Secure economic status of the family
☺   Good education (kindergarten, school)

☺ Appropriate parental education

☺ Communication in the family

☺ Reading to the child (fairy tales)

☺ Talking and listening to the child

☺ Learning atmosphere in the family

☺ Creative activities in the family

☺ Expressing interest in the child's emotional life

☺ Being truthful, reasonable and understanding

☺ Being reliable in all matters that affect the child

☺ Answering positively to the demand for attention

☺ Psychically and spiritually healthy parental relationship

☺ Parental caress and body touch influence the baby's brain development

Key early positive mental shaping processes that prepare for life:

❖ Self- and Life Management

❖ Managing the Family Relationship

- ❖ Moral, Belief and Spirituality

- ❖ Managing Personal Development

- ❖ Life Course of Working, Learning, Creating

- ❖ Politics, Governance, Economy

- ❖ Private and Public Education

- ❖ Care for Environment, Nature, Ecosystems

- ❖ Creating peace, justice, balance, hope

The state of the mind of people is highly shaped (constructed) by their biography and from inherent elements from previous generations. Most people in previous generations did not and do not have well shaped and developed mental functions. Nevertheless, people can also inherit positive experiences from these previous generations.

The first mental shaping processes, prenatal and the first 3-5 years, decisively form the foundation of a life course.

But there are concepts and methods to break free

from the burdens of the past. Early negative experiences can be cleaned out from the unconscious mind and replaced with alternative positive patterns.

## 2. MENTAL OPERATIONS

Mental functions are like "micro-chips" that need correctly programmed "software" to perform:

- Natural mental functions ("micro-chips") must be correctly nurtured ("programmed software")
- Each function must be trained, formed and developed for its specific use.
- Each function has a quality, efficiency, and meaning parameter.
- Underdeveloped and malformed or distorted functions have multiple negative effects.
- All functions are interrelated, influence each other and require multiple balances.

- Imbalance within and between functions leads to defective quality and critical effects.
- Effects of behavior are an expression of the high/low quality and high/low efficiency of the mental functions.

The shaped humans

- A human grows and develops with incoming information from many external and internal sources.
- People must become aware that most information from external realities is reduced, distorted or fabricated.
- People must learn the importance of the internal realities they perceive; they can learn to interpret them.

*The mind develops through manifold learning processes: high all-sided learning = high development.*

The 6 key developmental needs


- The Needs for the Mind

- The Needs for the Body

- The Needs for Life

- The Needs for Life Perspective

- The Needs for Constructive Behavior

- The Needs for Spirituality


People have all-encompassing spiritual needs


- Love for Life

- Skills for Life

- Zest and Skills for Work

- Self-Management Skills

- Meaningful Self-Realization

- Realization of Talents (Potentials)

- Happiness, Joy for Life

- Holistic Fulfillment

- Growing towards Completeness

- Interest in substantial Knowledge

- Truth, Truthfulness, Authenticity

The use of "spiritual Intelligence" (the mental function that creates dreams with messages) leads to fulfillment of the all-encompassing spiritual needs, which is the fundamental path for both individual and global evolution.

Nothing can be better in the world than the quality of the shaped minds

- Constructive behavior is rooted in the quality of the shaped mental functions.

- Constructive belief is the result of positive external influences since prenatal time, and for holistic growth.

- A constructive lifestyle is the result of external influences since prenatal time, and from a holistic growth.

The right way to shape the mental functions

Basically, the right way of shaping is in the genuine coding ("software") of the mental functions ("micro-chips") in the brain mass, programming correctly the determined potentials of all the mental functions and their multiple interrelations.

## 3. EVOLUTIONARY LIFE PHILOSOPHY

Evolutionary Philosophical Anthropology provides knowledge for:

- ❑ A new understanding of humans and evolution
- ❑ An evolutionary development for humanity
- ❑ Becoming responsible for personal growth
- ❑ The best possible fulfillment for people
- ❑ The most advanced positive Life Philosophy

The human creation

■ It is a unique gift to be a human, to be on earth, to make a living, and to grow lifelong.

■ Humans go through very different and unique life periods starting as an embryo.

■ The kinds of development are innumerable: biological, mental, spiritual, and behavioral.

■ The manifoldness of experiences humans can have during their life on earth is amazing.


Everything is like an organism


- It's senseless to think the 'other world' is in an eternally static state.

- Progression is meaningful, beneficial; regression is decadent and suicidal.

- Evolution shapes and serves humans, and is an intrinsic aim of all human life.

- Humans without evolution remain archaic, static, mulish, and ill-developed.

- Humanity moves between the direction of regression and evolution.

Everything is in endless development

- The planet with its ecosystems is in an endless complex evolutionary development.
- Societies are in an endless development, for either progression or regression.
- All humans are in an endless development either regressive or progressive.
- The community of all souls is in an endless development either regressive or progressive.

Practical life philosophy serves the human evolution

The fundamental intrinsic aim of humans and humanity is the achievement of (archetypal) psychical-spiritual evolution. Human evolution serves the People to develop their mind and soul for spiritual qualities. Human evolution also serves the souls in the other world for redemption. Human evolution serves the people in the future, the unborn today, and the generations for centuries to come.

*The present is the result of the past and the future is the result of the present and the past.*

Some practical aims of 'Evolutionary Life Philosophy'

■ To live, love, and fulfill the genuine psychical needs, with truthfulness

■ To acquire knowledge and skills and efficiently master life

■ To understand feelings and to be able to manage them

■ To prepare-people for a fulfilling relationship and family life

■ To live for and desire the other gender, for sex, for love and trust

■ To become free from unconscious biographical burdens

■ To be able to solve difficulties, crises, problems, conflicts

■ To care for health, nature, environment, and the planet

Human values are determined by human potentials. Some special examples are:

Self-consciousness. Mental. Hope. Fulfillment. Genuine life aims. Happiness about life. Satisfied sexuality. Pleasure and joy. Talents. Taking responsibility. Integrity. Morality. Love for the creation. Searching for the truth. Balanced judgment.

*There is an urgent need to put humanity on the track of the Archetypal Human Evolution. This will be explored and developed below.*

## 4. NEW WAYS OF LIVING

A new approach to a sustainable, successful, and fulfilling way of living

- Fulfilling ways of living provides success, happiness and fulfillment

- For a fulfilling life with periodic learning and renewal
- To take life into your own hands and shaping your own destiny

Methods and lifestyle

- Self-knowledge is a way of living and developing; it comes through training, practicing the methods. Each performance demands increased training.
- Meditation is a spiritual method which goes hand in hand with a lifestyle that gives time and space for the reflected and controlled management of the external life and the inner life.
- Practicing meditation and dream interpretation (meaning-oriented) don't go far without the use of other well formed psychical (mental) functions.

Basic suggestions

- To relax systematically and shortly twice a day (10 minutes)
- To write down the dreams daily when they can remember a dream
- To practice daily a short imagination exercise on any current issue
- To empty the mind each evening with a short mental-exercise
- During weekends to regularly spend an hour reflecting on the past week
- To read an enriching and stimulating book for a few hours a week

Live with your mind:

- Getting rid of inner suffering through analytical and contemplative elaboration
- Becoming free of conflicts, clarifying them and with the right attitudes
- Living requires a clear mind; means: balanced and doing 'things' at the right moment

- Dealing with life in a combination of analytical, artistic and creative way
- Thinking in an integrated combination of rationality and spirituality

Mental functions for ways of living

- To make a living, humans need well-formed psychical (mental) functions.
- Operational efficiency of the mind is an indispensable quality for success in life.
- Low efficiency of psychical functions leads to failure, critical results, and in the end to a failed life.
- To make a successful life, humans need to manage the quality of meaning (sense, values, importance).
- Low quality of meaning leads to failure, wrong results, and in the end to failure of life.

Self-management in everyday life

- A conscious and planned time organization is as important in private life as in the professional world.

- In the personal life (and not only at work) it is important to apply detailed planning to one's own goals.

- Creativity is essential for making a living. Individual problems can be solved more efficiently with creativity.

- To make a successful personal way of living, humans also need significant knowledge and skills.

- The ways of spending money fundamentally influence ways of managing life and happiness.

Health = Healthy Lifestyle

- 'Health' includes the whole human being with his lifestyle and psychical-spiritual and social being.

- Mental fitness includes intuition, imagination and spiritual experiences (experiencing meaning).

- Lifestyle includes a genuine identity, inner authenticity, realization (to give expression) of inner talents

- Lifestyle includes ability to control instinct and drive-satisfaction, also ability for living love.

## 5. NEW RELATIONSHIP MAN-WOMAN

The pattern of a relationship

- The relationship between man and woman is a kind of being with high values and a unique possibility of living with a managed personal psychical-spiritual development.

- Self-realization through a relationship is a particular challenge, because the patterns from childhood are repeated automatically by each adult.

- Two partners influence each other enormously in the development of their personality. The unconscious interplay is decisive for the superficially created ways of living together.

- ■ Masculinity and femininity are products in continuous processes of development, which are decisively influenced and transmitted socially. There are many ways of living masculine and feminine principles.

Partnership-like relationship

- ☑ Love in the partnership must be regularly stimulated and formed.
- ☑ Partnership regulates the common things by communication.
- ☑ The power-situation is balanced, and has to be worked at, daily.
- ☑ The partners don't possess each other with their whole being.
- ☑ The mutual dependence of sexual satisfaction is not against autonomy.

☑ Working out the unconscious life (the biography) is partly a shared activity.

☑ Partners orientate commonly on their dreams, intuitions and meditations.

Being a woman / Being a man

■ Man and woman: The psychical life as a wholeness 'functions' differently.

■ Masculine and feminine roles are not merely a product of learning processes.

■ Masculinity and femininity exist as a quality. That is linked psychically and physically.

■ Man and woman must bring in balance to the masculine and feminine principles

Man and woman are naturally (substantially) different

■ The psychical life (mind) as a whole doesn't work the same with men and women.

- Femininity and masculinity are psychological and biological qualities.

- No man and no woman can become 'complete' without the opposite gender.

- Man and woman have the psychical opposite gender as a polarity in their psyche.

- Creating a balanced 'male-female' wholeness is the essential characteristic of a marriage.

Meaning of marriage

'Marriage', in its core focuses archetypal inner processes; the meaning is 'archetypal-holy'; 'holy', because it is unimpeachable as an archetypal concept of the psyche (mind). Only through this aspect does 'marriage' as a ritual celebration and realization has full legitimacy. The 'homosexual or any other forms of marriage' have got nothing in common with this.

The promise of Love:

"I give my best for you and our life together; I guarantee with my mind and soul...":

☺ to understand you in your verbal and non-verbal expressions

☺ to support you and not to abuse your weaknesses

☺ to constructively deal with disagreements, arguments, misunderstanding

☺ to be a 'strong shoulder' for you when you need it and to encourage and assist you

☺ to satisfy your needs and desires in a way you feel comfortable with

☺ to balance my interests with your interests and to respect the rules of partnership

☺ to respect your qualities, feelings, and also your emotional limits

☺ to care for you and your being (mind, soul, heart, desires, body, health)

☺ to promote your psychological and spiritual development

☺ to respect and integrate all your qualities as a complementary part of mine

☺ to give highest priority to love and always to take care and nurture this love

## 6. MEDITATION AND CONTEMPLATION

Meditate in the appropriate manner

Meditation is visualization and an aim-oriented process operating with inner pictorial ideas. Firstly, always determine:

1. What do we want to achieve? Determination of aims. Reasoning.

2. With which images (symbols) do we want to work with? Determine instruments.

3. How do we actively create the visualization? Operations. Procedure.

4. How do we proceed with the interpretation? Interpretation.

5. How do we apply the result in daily life? Conclusions for life.

Imagination

- Imagination is the way of meditation (visualization) with the purpose of exploring, understanding and renewing (form, shape) the complete psychical and real life.
- With imagination one can relax, find new strength, prepare solutions for problems, free the mind from thoughts, understand other people, find the meaning of life, explore dreams, discover reasons for suffering and difficulties, explore the subconscious and much more.

Contemplation operates with archetypal symbols

- Archetypes are related to general patterns of psychical forces, to the processes of psychical transformation
- Archetypes reflect fundamental life themes, meaning and essential values, and the transcendental reality.

● Archetypes are for example: pyramids, mandalas, the sun, figures such as the old wise man (woman), and more.

● General symbols reflect the concrete basic themes of human existence, which concern all humans.

● General symbols are images from the real world: house, car, birth, marriage, child, old man, dog, mother, father, etc.

● Symbols (images) can express the essential real-life issues of everybody.

● Contemplation with Archetypes gives us a symbolical access to the "mystery" of mankind.


Examples to apply meditation


1)  Relaxation, balance and centering of energy

2)  Self-strengthening, renewing the energies

3)  Being conscious of one's daily life style

4)  To understand relationships

5)  Developing solutions for new challenges

6)  Clarifying difficulties and conflicts

7) Understanding psycho-somatic suffering

8) Getting rid of painful past experiences

9) Understanding dreams

10) Exploring all inner elements of the conscience

11) A conscious dealing with emotions (feelings)

12) Dealing with one's own needs

13) Strengthening will and ego-control

14) Recognizing projections and identifications

15) Using intelligence consciously

16) Broadening the perception

17) Understanding the mystery of mankind

18) Recognizing the state of the earth from a spiritual point of view

19) Identifying and understanding one's own destiny

20) Planning and realizing the path of Individuation.


## 7. DREAMS AND SPIRITUAL INTELLIGENCE

People have always given importance to dreams, although mostly with magic understanding. In the ancient world "big dreams" have been considered as messages from God. Today, for most people dreams do not have any importance for their life. There are also a lot of people that do not give any importance in thinking. People think dreams are rubbish.

Every human has dreams at night

- Every person dreams 2-4 times during his sleep. It's a human matter that many people can't remember their dreams. Everybody can learn to remember dreams.
- Dreams are not the rubbish of the everyday life or the past, or a result occurring by accident and without meaning. Dreams are a useful psychical-spiritual function.
- Images or sceneries in dreams can have a subjective or objective meaning, a spiritual meaning, an eternal meaning, the meaning of a behavior or an attitude; and some dreams express ritual processes of transformation.

The spiritual intelligence is a mental function (Spirit)

- ■ The spiritual intelligence is creating the dreams in order to guide humans.
- ■ The spiritual intelligence is 'talking' to the dreamer through dreams.
- ■ The spiritual intelligence operates in dreams aiming balance and development.
- ■ The spiritual intelligence is the only source to understand Soul and God (with dreams, meditation).
- ■ Humans can't manipulate dreams and can't manipulate the spiritual intelligence.
- ■ Correct interpretation requires knowledge about mind, behavior, world, life, etc.

Dreams tell the truth

- Dreams tell the truth about: dreamer, people, religions, ideologies, society, the planet, the future and God.

- 90% of all psychologists, therapists and analysts know a mere 10% about dreams and dream interpretation.
- Most people interpret their dreams on an archaic (magic) level (superstitious) with primitive knowledge.
- We can't interpret dreams correctly without knowledge about the unconscious and the real life.
- We need to grow psychologically and spiritually to understand our dreams correctly.

Dreams are the most valuable source of human existence

- Dreams inform, counsel, warn, support, promote, heal, develop, evaluate, and shape the evolutionary path.
- Dreams are an indispensable part of being human; shape the *"royal path"* to an entire psychical-spiritual universe.

- If this royal path is nurtured correctly, it enables us to reach the highest possible psychical-spiritual fulfillment.

The spiritual challenge for the archetypal human evolution

- We can manipulate and deform any mental function, any behavior, any individual, and any concept or knowledge. But we can never manipulate or deform the spiritual intelligence.
- The Spirit is not a human creation, not a product of culture, but a spiritual-psychical function in each psyche (soul, mind) of each human. The Spirit is the highest authority of human evolution

The spiritual challenge for religions and concepts of spirituality

- Religion without the spiritual intelligence, without dreams and the Archetypes of the Soul is archaic and useless, a fabrication, and destroys humanity and the archetypal human evolution.

- The inner Spirit (the spiritual intelligence) is the highest authority and stands above all religions and concepts of governance, above all dogmatic and ideological teaching!

Dreams determine human evolution

Dreams also must be integrated in life coaching, spiritual teaching, psycho-analytical theories and practices, and in philosophical thinking about the human being and human existence, and in real life and personal development.

*In the future, the new breed of leaders will integrate and use the spiritual intelligence in order to solve the global mess and to bring humanity on the track of the archetypal human evolution.*

# 8. SPIRITUALITY AND MEANING

To be human and to grow as a human is immanently spiritual.

- The word 'spiritual' refers to meaning and human values, human qualities, qualities of the soul and of life.
- Soul, mind, transcendental roots and terrestrial life can't be separated without losing psychical-spiritual growth.
- Genuine human values and inner needs are spiritual
- The ability to love is a spiritual function
- The meaning of all human interactions is spiritual
- Searching for the meaning of life is spiritual
- To forgive, reconcile, learn, and renew is spiritual
- Joy of life and genuine happiness are spiritual
- Peace has an inherent spiritual meaning
- Fulfillment in life is a spiritual aim of human's life

- Love between a man and woman is especially spiritual
- Marriage has a deep spiritual and archetypal meaning
- Inner archetypal processes are spiritual and psychological
- Catharsis of the unconscious mind is a spiritual process
- Creating balance between the different mental systems is spiritual
- Growing towards wholeness is a psychological and a spiritual process
- Spiritual qualities require quality and efficiency of all psychical functions
- The 'mission' that every person (soul) immanently has, is to become higher 'qualities', means to become 'complete' through a terrestrial life.
- It becomes obvious that soul, mind, transcendental roots and terrestrial life can't be separated without losing the psychical-spiritual development.

- The psychical-spiritual development is the fundamental challenge to become 'round', complete and fulfilled as a human and a soul. There is no other way!

The Circle-Cross Symbol has an intrinsic meaning

Becoming and being a human, aim of human life, love, joy, zest for life, happiness, hope, justice, peace, power of the inner Spirit, totality, completeness, balance, openness, and psychical-spiritual evolution aiming fulfillment. The crucifix contains the opposite values: pure frightening darkness. Human Evolution is based on archetypal life symbols.

**The Life Symbol: Genuine Source of Life**

Intrinsic meaning: Human being, life, love, joy, zest for life, lust, full of life, satisfaction, happiness, hope, justice, peace, power of the inner Spirit, centered in the inner Spirit, all-embracing life, totality, completeness, balance, openness, light, confidence, aim, psychical-spiritual evolution, fulfillment, conjunction of the real and spiritual world, fulfillment of the Archetypes of the Soul, source of life, catharsis, renewal, reconciliation, forgiveness, salvation, redemption, and presence of God.

Spirituality is the innermost stream of values which characterize the genuine human evolution as a transcendental-terrestrial project. With this new understanding, spirituality must become an indispensable innermost stream of politics, economy, public and academic education, and religion for the future of humanity and the future ways of living. This is an archetypal order and the fundamental principle of the genuine human evolution.

# 9. EVOLUTIONARY EDUCATION

- Education about psychical-spiritual development is fundamental for the youth and for all adults, including new ways of living and understanding of mankind and human life.
- New spiritual education is also required for all people in responsible positions in politics, media, economy, industry, education, and religion.

Importance of new education

- Highest importance as education is the fundamental preparation for success in life, work, and renewal in a very fast changing world. Pioneering vocational education is fundamental.
- The immense problems of humanity and the planet can't be solved without fundamental renewal of education and especially a fundamental revision and re-construction of economics.

- Constructive behavior in life, in social life, in political participation, in the world of work and business must become subjects and topics of science.

- Holistic and permanent all-embracing psychical-spiritual development aiming for inner satisfaction and fulfillment must become subjects and topics of science.

- Inner rooted spirituality, moral integrity, meaning of life, respect for humanity, nature, animals and the protection of the planet and its ecosystems.


New mission of public education


- Public Education must be founded on a new understanding of mankind and human life.

- Public Education must consider a holistic forming of all mental functions.

- Public Education must focus on the inner psychical-spiritual process.

- Public Education must teach that 'meaning' is intrinsically part of being a human.

- Public Education must prepare people for resolving problems and conflicts.

- Public Education must provide the knowledge of money-, self- and time-management.

- Public Education must shape the genuine human values and its practical capacities.

- Public Education must promote critical and creative or pioneering thinking.

- Public Education must teach extensively the manifold capacities of the power of love.

- Public Education must integrate the potentials of spiritual intelligence (dreams, meditation).


Global need for new education


- Billions of people need knowledge, skills or methods to understand themselves and their life, their difficulties, their problems and conflicts.

- Billions of people must be protected from brainwashing, manipulation, evil seductions, false games, and the perverse and neurotic collective theater of public life.
- Billions of people must be enabled to live love and to be loved, to find happiness and satisfaction, to create success and a secure life environment.

Self-knowledge is fundamental in Public Education (all levels)

*Self-knowledge is the call for all humans to be and to become a genuine human - a mission also for public education.*

- Self-knowledge forms qualification for personal and professional life.
- Self-knowledge establishes competences for relationships and life.
- Self-knowledge reduces life risks and suffering over the life course.

■ Self-knowledge creates inner security and trust in one's own forces.

■ Self-knowledge forms an all-sided balanced person (personality).

*Private (public) education including social sciences, schools of business and economics, must be 100% free from accreditation requirements. This is an absolute must in order to find collectively back the archetypal human evolution.*

## 10. ARCHETYPAL PERSONAL DEVELOPMENT

Each holistic psychical-spiritual development, we call it "Individuation" or "Individuation Process", aims to become a 'fulfilled human'.

Archetypes of the Soul

- Archetypes are symbols that help in finding orientation during the process of Individuation.

- Archetypes stimulate forces, growth and development; above all the truth of human evolution.

- Archetypes order and place psychical functions into new structures and new interconnections.

- Archetypes give orientation for humanity, religion, spirituality, politics, economy, and education.

- Archetypes are eternally valid meaning about human being, meaning of life, and fulfillment.

- Archetypes can never be extinguished, are 'holy', 'untouchable', and valid for all humans forever.

_**Growing continuously and evolutionarily, psychologically and spiritually, is called 'Individuation':**_

Archetypes give measures (standards) in quality and quantity, embedded in human life.

- Archetypes are like laws and norms or 'milestones' for the psychical-spiritual development.

- Archetypes call for personal development and competences for living (knowledge, skills).

- Archetypes reflect transcendental realities in the psyche and realities in the other world.

- Archetypes are the very old images of a transcendental reality, the eternal valid orientation.

- ■ Archetypes of the Soul are also energetic 'transformers' (e.g. to experience in dreams).

*There are since millenniums supreme Archetypes of the Soul which are related to high professional 'missions'. Such eternally infallible symbols are also today valid, obviously with modern knowledge and frame of life. They express the spiritual preparations for power and destination of a spiritual king, a prophet, a religious leader, and of political or economic leadership (head of states, ministers, and CEOs).*

*Humanity needs a new breed of leaders that have processed such supreme Archetypes.*

# The Schellhammer Archetypal Pyramid
# The Development of Human Needs

## (small text edition)

**Third Age Needs:**

Fulfilled Path of Development

Living the Archetypes of the Soul

**Senior Age 51-65 year Needs:**

Higher Inner Development

Mission for the Collective

**Adult Age 36-50 year Needs:**

Strong Mental Functions for Life and Work

Reached Completeness and Fulfillment

**Young Adult 19-35 year Needs:**

Self-responsible for Inner Development

Genuine Self-realization, Learning for Work and Life

**Adolescence 13-18 year Needs:**

Becoming Self-responsible, Shaping Self-identity

Self-knowledge, Genuine Human Values

### Ages 7-12 year Needs:

Development of the Mind, Self-discovering

Exploring Worlds, Adaptation of Rules


### Ages 4-6 year Needs:

Understanding and Managing Emotions

Communication, Mental and Physical Stimuli


### Ages 1-3 year Needs:

Opportunities for Learning and Explorations

Healthy Life for Mental and Social Development


### Prenatal Needs:

Caring Environment, Healthy Nutriments

Healthy Emotional-mental State of the Mother


## <u>Basic Needs for the Lifespan of ALL Humans:</u>

Healthy Food, Water, Air, Environment, Shelter, Security, Protection, Care, Health Care, Learning, Work, Money for Living, Responsibility, Education, Inner Development, Justice, Peace, Ethics, Hope, Love, Truth, Knowledge, Human Values, Meaning, Sexuality, Genuine Spirituality, Evolving Capacities

<u>Changes through New Ways of Living</u>:

Everybody can contribute to catharsis and renewal of life, of the world and humanity:

1. Promote a lot your self-knowledge and psychical-spiritual development
2. Elaborate your biography and get rid of unsolved passed conflicts and pain
3. Learn how to efficiently solve conflicts, problems, difficulties and crises
4. Chose a partner that shares with you growing and living with the soul
5. Learn through courses before getting married and procreating
6. Daily write down your dreams and learn and practice dream interpretation
7. Respect your energy and biorhythm and live with smart self-management
8. Talk daily minimum an hour (average) with your partner and your children

9.   Learn to correctly meditate and meditate daily twice 10-15 minutes

10.  Never stop asking questions about life, love, trust, hope, belief and the truth

11.  Live always rooted in the genuine human values and the Archetypes of the Soul

12.  Buy a car only when you absolutely need it for business or going to work

13.  Don't drive around with your car just for fun or for a bit of shopping

14.  Always buy a car with cash and never with a loan or leasing or renting

15.  Consume 30-40% less petrol (by driving less, driving with care)

16.  Use public transport whenever you can and accept walking up to 30 minutes

17.  Reduce by 30% the amount of meat and fish that you consume

18.  Use 20% less water (shower, washing, cleaning, garden, etc.)

19. Reduce lightening, heating, A/C and appliances by 30% (electricity, oil, gas)

20. Moderation if necessary: Smoke 50% less and / or drink 50% less alcohol

21. Use your credit/debit card only when you really need to; at least 75% less

22. Get cash from the bank or the ATM of your bank (buy everything with cash)

23. Pay off all your credit card debt every end of the month

24. Buy 50% less soda/beer/wine (alternatively drink tea at home)

25. Buy local products such as vegetables, fruits, meat, fish, bakery products

26. Buy 75% less newspapers, junk magazines, stationery articles (paper, ink)

27. Go on holiday in foreign countries only every 2-5 years; avoid mass tourism

28. Perfume/Toiletry: use 20-30% less (simply do not exaggerate the use)

29. Avoid getting a loan for consumption (work first and save to get later what you want)

30. Buy 90% less pre-prepared (frozen) meals (cook your own meals)

31. Use detergents sparingly and medicine (psychotropic) when it is appropriate only

32. Turn off appliances at home (TV, PC, Radio, etc.) when not used

33. Watch 50-80% less TV every day and examine the value of the content

34. Reduce waste by 50% (package, plastic, newspaper, magazines, paper, etc.)

35. Use the dishwasher and washing machine only when it's appropriate

36. Use your mobile phone or smart phone and computer (Internet, Facebook) 75% less

37. Buy natural and creative toys for your kids and never (plastic) gadgets with batteries

38. Contract mortgages only with a low interest rate and at least 10-year fixed rate

39. Buy a home with at least 50% cash; never buy a holiday home with a mortgage

40. Contract insurance policies with a certain amount of own risk

41. Don't speculate (lottery, gambling, casino, investments, bets, etc.)

42. Go to shopping centers only when there is no local alternative for what you want

43. Every month, buy a book that improves your work, business, life and personality

44. Buy quality goods (products) considering their long-term sustainability (value)

45. Buy decorations from local artists (handicrafts) and only local seasonal flowers

46. Eat moderately sweeties, chocolate and snacks and maximum once a week

47. All kind of drugs (cocaine, heroin, soft drugs, etc.) are absolutely taboo

48. If you have a garden, use some space for a vegetable and berry garden

49. Plant on your terrace or garden a lot of seasonal flowers and herbs

50. Spend part of your leisure for sport, creative activities (e.g. painting, handicraft)


➡ *Either humanity finds new evolutionary ways of living, or Armageddon will be unavoidable!*


## CONSTITUTION OF ARCHETYPAL EVOLUTION

### A. GOD IS EVERYTHING

God is the fountainhead of all life; and God is also the Spirit. Each human soul is created from this fountainhead and lives in eternal development. Value, promote and form the human being and the all-sided balanced human life; live and grow from your inner being with the inner Spirit (spiritual intelligence) and with love.


### B. ONLY GOD IS GOD

You shall not abuse God or the Spirit for egoistic and

compensatory purposes, or greed for power, self-enhancement, exploitation of humans and the earth. Nobody is entitled to ban or condemn humans in the name of God. Jurisdiction in the spiritual world is solely and exclusively reserved for a true Messiah and the spiritual kings in the world of the souls.

## C. YOUR LIFE AND AIM

Regularly take enough time to contemplate about you, your life, your fellow human beings, humanity and the earth. The highest aim in your life is to aspire and to live your all-sided balanced completeness in the evolutionary development. A human is a human through his psychical-spiritual organism. Herein lies begin and aim of the human evolution.

## D. MARRIAGE AND FAMILY

The marriage between man and woman is untouchable and shall not be abused. Dignify being father and being mother as a high value of being and living. To educate a child is a demanding responsibility that requires formation, and has to be embedded in the polarity of man and woman as a couple, or in individual cases as a kinsman like or friendship like community.


## E. VIOLENCE AND PUNISHMENT

You shall not be violent against humans or kill humans. A state has never got the right to kill a human as punishment (or for political interests) or to violate humans physically or psychically; not even in the frame of a persecution or investigation. You also shall not provoke other humans in such a way or put them in a desperate situation so that they become violent.


## F. LOVE AND SEXUALITY

Live your genuine physical and psychical needs in a balanced and healthy way. Do not act against love or the inner Spirit. You shall not devalue the natural sexual needs, nor suppress them, nor live them in a perverted way. Live your sexuality with your opposite gender partner in a human way and with love. Do not create a baby if you are not prepared and not mature for the consequences, educationally and financially.

## G. PROPERTY RIGHT AND POWER

Do not exploit (abuse) humans and institutions. You shall not take away from other people or from institutions or from other countries what is their right to possess. Humans, economy and states do not have the right to exhaustively exploit resources. No human, no institution and no government shall have enough power to create a national or global imbalance. Jurisdiction requires fairness, transparency, balance, justice, free from feudalistic spirit.

## H. AUTHENTICITY AND RESPONSIBILITY

Acknowledge yourself and love yourself. From this state love the human being. You shall not make a wrong image of yourself. You shall not ignore, suppress or displace the realities with the purpose of gaining advantage or damaging humans or institutions. You shall not cheat others. You shall never abuse political, economic, and religious or media power.

## I. SOCIAL STRUCTURE

Society, states and humanity shall be created and developed in the attitudes of love and rooted in the inner Spirit, in a way that each human can realize his psychical-spiritual potentials and grow in a protected life frame. It is an absolute imperative from God that society and humanity shall not be militarized.

## J. EARTH AND ITS NATURE

Protect with your way of living the nature, the richness of the earth and its resources in the interest of the community of humans and the genuine human needs – also for the future generations. In the interest of the conservation of the earth and of human evolution, all folks shall live with highest regard for the psychical-spiritual values and the vivid Archetypes of the Soul.

## FINAL WORDS

There are countless scientists and institutions that strongly warn all: A very dark millennium is looming. Human evolution is at stake! The total collapse could occur within 10-20 years.

People have to clean up the mess themselves! There are less than 4-5 years left to implement first strong changes. What happens today, will affect humanity in 5, 10 or more years.

It will take 25 years to establish the genuine (archetypal) path of human evolution.

I came to earth 2,000 years ago and again in the 12$^{th}$ century in Spain. Both divine missions failed terribly. Now, I was ordered to come back again. I didn't like it at all.

*I have all power of attorney from God as the highest judge of all souls on this planet and in the other world.*


People must change or the destruction of human evolution will occur. You want peace, justice, balance and hope; then you must make it! People must change and renew for their evolution.

If the heads of governments, religions, and mass media hinder me to do my job, and if they do not support my pioneering divine project, I will send these souls into a dark place, far from God and his light for 50,000 years.

Leaders in all systems of society must manage changes and renewal towards archetypal human evolution. If they reject to do so, their soul must expect to get 10,000 - 30,000 years of being far from

God and his light.

The all-powerful string-pullers behind the curtains will get 100,000 years 'dark hole' if they do not immediately change their Deicide program into collective archetypal human evolution.
If human evolution will be entirely destroyed, I will send all souls into a dark place, far from God and his light for 200,000 years.

I can guide you. I can give you absolution for the entire evil past and present. But this must be based on sustainable results of actions. Human evolution must be established with the 'Archetypes of the Soul'.

**As a measure of discipline, I have closed the door to Paradise for all souls - with some exceptions - until the complete enlightenment of the truth is achieved globally.**

*Schellhammer Education provides you with the indispensable knowledge, education, advice and guidance.*

**Document of Highest Archetypal Processes of the Soul**

(Extract from Dr. Edward Schellhammer, "The Manifesto")

Dream: *"Find the mystery of mankind!"* somebody invited me.

Dream: An owl is guiding me.

Dream: Out of my abdomen a little tree grows.

Dream: I receive a sword, a sceptre, a globe and a cross; these symbols I compose into a circle-cross-Mandala.

Dream: I am in various churches, in ecclesiastical

libraries looking for the truth. What I find is a lot of dust and stones.

Dream: I experience a ritual: *"God nourishes you, God strengthens you, God protects you, and God guides you."*

Dream: I go to the Valley of the Kings with seven white elephants.

Dream: I receive a goblet and I am summoned to search the mysteries of life in it.

Dream: I'm able to draw the sword of the king of the Grail from the rock and then I'm given an orb.

Dream: The ruler of the collective unconscious world of souls points his finger at me and shouts: *"This is the new Messiah!"*

Dream: I'm unified with this light; I am one with this

sun. *"This is the unio mystica"* I hear said.

Dream: Preparations for a celebration "accomplishment of the Individuation process" is made.

Dream: Within me is the temple of the Holy Grail. Actually, I know everything.

Dream: A voice: *"He, the Individuated man, has a particular assignment in this world, only thought (made) for him. Only he is worthy for it since he is the man of God, the third in the covenant with God and the Spirit."*

Dream: *"You know how life grows. You are life. You are being. You only do what you are. You come from the source in God. You understand the primal source of life. The people want bread from you"*, somebody says.

Dream: I've reached the goal. I've got the water and the fire and I know the path and the goal.

Dream: *"You know that God does not go to man, man has to seek God. God is life, wisdom and love. God is within you; you are in God. The signet ring is guaranteed to you. You are the king. You are the trustee of a concern which is not of this world. The new man is born.*

Dream: Through the fog I see the future. More and more people get ill and die.

Dream: The president of the USA has allowed me to tell him one of my dreams in front of the plenary assembly, and so I speak: "I saw a king coming to Europe, as pure and clear as none before. And I saw that all the nations disarmed; and I saw, how the king brought peace to all people on earth, the peace from God." Suddenly I realize I am talking about myself.

Dream: The Spirit says: "You are appointed and ready: The Messiah is great and alive. You have got the proper equipment to face the world."

Dream: I experience, that I have passed all the ordeals (trials) in the union with God.

Dream: The inner Spirit speaks to me: "You represent God on earth. Nobody else! You have got all the powers of attorney. Make use of them. You are a true king of the Holy Grail. The world of souls is your kingdom. God loves you very much."

Dream: One of a group of spectators shouts out repeatedly: "This is truly the reincarnated Messiah, have mercy upon us." Then all of them pray this in a chorus.

Dream: The evil, a figure of horror, approaches me and says: "And you're playing the second leading part."

Dream: I receive 'cosmic scissors' and with them I cannot only cut and separate, but also join together and create wholeness.

Dream: I receive a new signet ring with twelve gemstones. "This is the ring of the Messiah" it is said.

Dream: I am wearing the signet ring: "No one dares to wear this ring and the last one who did, was living 2000 years ago."

Dream: Those, who perpetrate atrocities against the values of love and the Spirit, are severely punished in the spiritual world.

Dream: A king has got two pharaoh birds, very colourful and marvellously beautiful. It is said that these are magic birds. We come to the city of Jerusalem. I'm very glad we've finally reached the goal together with the kingly birds.

Dream: The Reincarnated Christ has got a unique relationship with the sun: He carries it on his hands, but it is also within him, he calls it and gives it to the people whenever they want it.

Dream: The punishment is pronounced and sealed. Only the reincarnated Messiah can annul it. No folk can ignore his Messiah without the gravest consequences for the collective.

Dream: I am in the Vatican, in an immense arch room, full of all kinds of junk. There is absolutely nothing here that could have a value or could be vivid.

Dream: The whole project is finished. Everything is ready; I and my matters; for the whole humanity.

Dream: I walk through the Vatican. And I ask myself

who has paid and still pays for all this, and under which conditions has all this been built. Hidden behind all of this is an immeasurable megalomania, a perverse suppression and exploitation.

Dream: A voice is speaking: "You are the new Messiah of humanity, and the guarantee for a good future."

Dream: I tell people: "Never again will I come back to this earth. I am only here for a visit and I have to accomplish a job. And you have to get your shit together yourself."

Dream: I tell the press: "You haven't got the slightest clue about what kind of punishment is waiting for you for having ignored me and having kept me from the people!"

Dream: "I have not come from millions of light years away to this earth, sent from God, to play here the cretin and idiot.

Dream (2008): I told people in a dream: "You have 10 years left to take strong measures to avoid the total collapse." But nobody listens. (That means in 2011: You have got 7 years left!)

Dream (2010): In 35-40 years everything will be over, the end, no more earth and no more humanity.

Dream (2015): The end of human evolution could be already in 20 years.

**Therefore, with all the power of attorney from my spiritual (archetypal) authority I decide today:**

Year 2014: I have closed the door to the paradise. I will not let a single soul into Paradise, apart from a few exceptions, until the evil octopus on this planet is detected and disclosed, until the truth is researched and clarified and until both are fully understood by the entire humanity. Everyone is summoned to work on this catharsis and renewal: Researchers, experts, scientists, journalists, politicians, legal professionals, CEOs, and all kinds of power holders and religious officials; <u>but also, all humans being in a state to contribute in any ways to this catharsis and renewal.</u>

Every single person must be educated with the path that leads towards the fulfillment of the Archetypes of the Soul: the all-encompassing catharsis and the psychical-spiritual educational process, guided by the inner Spirit and the power of love. The day, one billion adults work on this process, I will re-open for these people the door to Paradise.

## THE FOUNDER

Dr. Edward Schellhammer is the founder and President of the Schellhammer Education Group that includes the Schellhammer Business School, the Schellhammer Institute and the Schellhammer Retreat.

What is most striking about meeting Dr. Edward Schellhammer beyond his pleasant and polite manner; youthful disposition or passionate and sincere views on humanity and the planet, is his unshakable conviction that the world needs a new pioneering education.

But exactly who is Dr. Edward Schellhammer? Is he a Philosopher, an expert on human matters, a Psychologist, a prolific author of over 30 titles from psychology to politics and economics, an educator, or a visionary with a profound and beneficial insight into the human condition?

The answer is that he is all that and more. In different age, he would have been called a polymath, and probably kept close company with those giants of The Age of Enlightenment, like his fellow countryman Jean Jacques Rousseau, Thomas Payne and perhaps even Thomas Jefferson. For, it is exactly this gift of enlightenment that Dr. Schellhammer wants to give humanity.

He reveals: "My studies, global travels, professional experiences and extensive study and research since 1970 have given me a clear and unique insight into humanity, human evolution, spirituality, education, cultures, needs, values, standards and our purpose in life like no other!"

Pausing to add: "Humanity hasn't even begun to discover what the true path of human life on earth is fundamentally good and right for".

Born and educated in Switzerland he has lived in

Paris, South of France, London, Kiel, Detroit, and Mexico, before settling in Marbella, Spain, some 27 years ago.

He studied Education, Psychology, Psychoanalysis, and Philosophy. He was a lecturer at the University of Zurich as well as other institutions, and as a member of international workshops he dedicated his ample energy to futurology, future perspectives of humanity, peace and disarmament, development of education in Latin America and key global issues in general, concentrating on developing a new understanding of politics and economics for the future. His findings are indispensable for all those who value life, love, and justice.

He places great emphasis on Dream Theory a subject that he has researched for most of his life and passionately believes in, declaring that some 35 years ago he had a dream that told him to solve the mystery of man and human evolution. Stating categorically: "My initial reaction was, this is an impossible task!" and then quickly adds with equal conviction: "But today, I think, no, I know, that I have discovered all the fundamental components that explain the mystery of man and human evolution."

With his professional background, he has written many books spanning: Individuation (holistic personal development), Dream Theory and Interpretation, Problem Solving, The Individual and Collective Unconscious, Love and Relationships, The Archetypes of Man, The Future of Humanity, Global Human Education, New Philosophical Anthropology, Didactics in Teaching and Counseling and Coaching.

All inner processes – psychical, spiritual and practical – to find and live the (archetypal) codes of human evolution are well documented like never before in the history of mankind. Everything that you need to learn is elaborated in his books.

Dr. Edward Schellhammer has unveiled the mystery of mankind, the psychological-spiritual and archetypal codes of human evolution. It has taken 35 years to understand humans, the divine and factual human evolution, the mendacious aims of politics, economy, public education, religion, spirituality, and the state of humanity and the world, in order to offer you today the eternally valid concept (codes) of the Archetypal Human Evolution.

During the last 35 years he had around 14,000 dreams about the state and development of humanity, the world and the planet. Countless dreams have shown him everything of fundamental relevance for humanity's future and evolution.

During the same period, he also had estimated 3,000 dreams about the genuine archetypal evolution of mankind, the state and potentials of the mind and of the world population, the 'other world' and God. He has been in his dreams in the 'other world', in the divine paradise, and he has experienced the 'Union with God' as well as many more archetypal processes. He profoundly elaborated all this; estimated 80,000 hours of explorations and analysis in total.

Dr. Edward Schellhammer says: "The never achieved most advanced psychological, spiritual, archetypal, educational and practical concept, the Philosophical Anthropology of the Archetypal Human Evolution, is prepared and can lead humanity to hope, peace, justice, balance, truthfulness, and fulfillment."

Like the man himself his books are not for the faint hearted with challenging, pioneering and vanguard content and new ways of thinking that covers shaping of the mind, personal development, human values, human evolution, life, business, politics, economy, society, education, and religion – for everybody that is searching for the truth and for a fundamental personal fulfillment. Reading his books is pure adventure for the mind.

After decades of extensive explorations, research, analysis, writing and sometimes personal retreat, Dr. Edward Schellhammer is now at the disposal of discerning individuals and institutions wishing to pursue prepared and tailor-made programs of evolutionary further education.

HUMANITY NEEDS A NEW CONCEPT FOR 'MANKIND', A NEW SPIRITUALITY, AND A NEW BREED OF EVOLUTIONARY HUMANS!

HUMANITY NEEDS A NEW GENERATION OF ALL-ROUND PREPARED LEADERS IN EVERY FIELD OF HUMAN ENDEAVOR!

HUMANITY NEEDS A NEW CONCEPT OF BUSINESS SCHOOLS, OF UNIVERSITIES, AND OF A NEW PUBLIC EDUCATION!

HUMANITY NEEDS TO RECLAIM THE ARCHETYPAL SPIRITUALITY ('RELIGION') THAT WAS NEVER ESTABLISHED IN THE PAST!

17.04.2011 I dreamt: "The door to Paradise must now be completely closed for all souls, until the complete enlightenment of the truth is fulfilled globally." Therefore, with all the power of attorney from my spiritual (archetypal) authority [that has given it to me in dreams] and in order to save the human evolution I decide today:

I will not let a single soul into Paradise, apart from a few exceptions, until the deicide octopus is detected and disclosed, until the truth is researched and clarified and put on the table, and until both are fully understood by the entire humanity. Everyone is summoned to work on this catharsis and renewal: Researchers, experts, scientists, journalists, politicians, legal professionals, CEOs, and all varieties of power holders and religious officials; but also, all and every single citizen of all states and nations.

"As the highest judge of all souls living in the other world and of all souls living today and in the future on this earth, I will severely punish the supreme masters of deicide with a minimum of 50,000 years being far away from God and his light, the protagonists with a minimum of 10,000 years, and all other significant collaborators of deicide will not see God and his light for a very long time. People that are unwilling to learn and to develop themselves psychically and spiritually and those who infect the collective (entire societies) with brainwashing, lies and falseness, with their insane narcissism, perverse neurosis, psychosis, psychopathy and madness cannot expect to be allowed to enter into paradise. It is said since millenniums: If a folk and its government ignore its new (genuine, provable) prophet, destroy his life, bans him, and paralyzes with that his divine mission for humanity and the archetypal human evolution, this folk will lose its land. Switzerland is already sentenced. The same punishment is applied for any folk that acts in the same way against this prophet for humanity in the third Millennium. If all of humanity accepts the deicide simply by ignoring it, then most souls will be sent for 200,000 years to a dark place far away from the paradise of God."

## THE FOUNDATION FOR A NEW LIFE

THE MANIFESTO (ISBN: 1494855917): The book unveils the state of people, of humanity, of the world and the planet. People destroy the evolution of humanity with their blinded religious, atheist or other mental or political insanity. The Manifesto puts the challenge on the table, as never before! Not wanting to know is a shame. How can you be happy with a suppressed shame? You can only become free inside with knowledge, critical thinking, and self-contemplation. This book tells you the 'truth' about the world and the lost archetypal path of humanity!

ARMAGEDDON OR EVOLUTION (ISBN: 1484868668): There are only two options: Humanity's leaders take responsibility to manage evolution in a sustainable manner, or the systemic fissures will crush mankind and the planet will degenerate. The book reveals how everybody can contribute to a sustainable human life. Why should you have a good life if you don't contribute for a better world? The book contains all you need to know about the species called 'human': fulfilling ways of living, evolutionary personality development, man-woman-relationship aiming for 'completeness', a substantial advanced philosophy about humans, and a realistic overview of the big problems around the globe.

THE FUTURE IN YOUR HANDS (ISBN: 1478377917): The truths and facts are outrageous and beyond all imagination. The damages worldwide are monstrous. Everybody pays with their taxes during centuries for ignoring the ongoing massive destruction and wars. Nevertheless, everybody can contribute to create a new path for humanity. The state of humanity and the world - preprogrammed from previous generations - shows us that most parents don't care about what the future will bring to their children. If parents don't care about the future of their children, then the young generation must learn to take their future into their own hands!

DEICIDE (ISBN: 1478366524): Indicted: The supreme masters of neo-capitalism, the leaders of corporations, banks, politics, media, justice, the ultra-high net worth individuals, the leaders of education, universities, Christianity; humans that destroy the genuine human values and that accept the lies as the truth. Those who seriously want to understand the mess also get the conceptual solutions. A must read for all those who work in the education sector, in politics, economy or religion.

BECOME A STRONG PERSONALITY (ISBN: 1478372958): The book provides everything that all people must develop for a sustainable inner foundation in order to be prepared for a fast-changing world. It is ridiculous and stupid if you do not want to become a genuine, strong personality. Read this to prepare yourself for the world!

LOVE YOUR LIFE (ISBN: 1478372834): Everybody needs to build up the ability to love, and to live joy of life. The book provides everything that must be developed in order to find happiness. Most people do not have the slightest idea what love is about. It's much more than an emotion. A must for anyone interested in genuine love!

60 DAYS TO PARADISE (ISBN: 1480177369): Everybody needs to learn about how to develop a better life. The book provides countless tips and practical suggestions to reach genuine success. The paradise is within you. Therefore: Do you want darkness and the hell inside or the eternal sun? You will find out how to create your inner sun.

PRACTICAL PSYCHOLOGY (ISBN: 147836694X): The book provides immense knowledge about humans, human life and human concerns; countless exercises promote personal development, a better life, and professional competences in matters of human life. 90-95% of all humans are archaic humans like people who lived 1000 and 2000 years ago. It is really urgent that you evolve with this book to a very valuable inner status of quality and being.

PSYCHOLOLGY I (ISBN: 1478370661): This book expands the frame of 'Practical Psychology' and presents more precise knowledge about matters of human life and the mind. A lot of practical exercises allow one to reach a high level of genuine personal development. Read rubbish and live with delusions. Remain ignorant. Or take this book in your hands and start becoming a complete and fulfilled human with a precious soul and efficient mind.

POLITICS (ISBN: 1480198714): Politics has failed in

achieving peace on earth, in eliminating the roots of all wars, in creating economic balance, and in promoting human evolution. Outrageous failure! The world needs 10 million and more new politicians and leaders with all-encompassing advanced knowledge and the right personal development. Before you talk about politics and leadership, read this book!

ECONOMICS I (ISBN: 1478226730): The book unveils the dogma and ideology of the biggest scam in modern history that led to the degradation of humanity and the planet via 'profits at all costs'. All business people and those who work in a field of the economy must know what the academic education does not tell you. If you don't want to know, you are a collaborator of the collective destruction.

ECONOMICS II (ISBN: 1478244577): The book delves into the key elements of microeconomics and their intricate relation to financial crises and the omnipresent destructivity exerted on humanity. This book teaches you what you will not learn in accredited economic teaching. Become a robot and servant of the capitalist cynicism or learn about the lies and scams for a new economic world.

ECONOMICS III (ISBN: 1478275626): The book uncovers key facts and figures of the state of humanity and the planet; revealing herewith the systemic failures in economics, politics, education and religion. Not wanting to know about the roots of failures in the economy, in politics, education and religion serves the hidden masters, which systematically destroy the archetypal (genuine) human development. Therefore: Expand your view and serve the human development!

MODERN DREAM THEORY (ISBN: 1478384891): Dreams guide people to the truth, to the power of the inner Spirit. Dream form the ethical, psychological, spiritual and religious foundation of life. Dream shed light on all the principles of the psychical-spiritual growth. Without the 'Spiritual intelligence' of dreams, people can never find fulfillment. There is no better guidance for everyone, regardless of culture, religion or ideology. There is no future for humanity, without taking the power of the inner Spirit seriously.

200 WAYS TO SAVE THE PLANET (ISBN: 1548039209): "Humanity has 25 years left to implement relevant and all-encompassing changes, but must start now." Herein, Dr. Schellhammer outlines 200 concrete ways of practical change for every human being around the globe that can guarantee a change from the cataclysmic roller coaster ride that humanity finds itself on today to a complete renewal in order to bring humanity "back to the path of (archetypal) genuine human evolution," he says.

> *All books available worldwide on Amazon, in paperback and Kindle version. For German versions, see schellhammerinstitut.com.*

# SCHELLHAMMER RETREAT

The Schellhammer Retreat is an educational institution that offers a one-of-a-kind Retreat together with a unique self-development educational program. The Schellhammer Retreat is about discovery, spirituality, fulfillment and self-exploration through the process of Individuation. Participants are offered a breakthrough in their personal life, fulfillment in their vocation, a deeper archetypal meaning of life, an inner catharsis, and the complete absolution.

The Schellhammer Retreat is a psychical-spiritual 'Life School' that can lead individuals to high and very high aims of the Individuation Process. It includes the shaping processes of any kind of mission for humanity and the genuine (archetypal) human evolution.

*Book yourself a stay: SchellhammerRetreat.com.*